COMPACT
CYMRU

CH00530328

...ce Names
Explained

ed: Myrddin ap Dafydd

Gwasg Carreg Gwalch

First published in 2016

© images:
Marian Delyth
Pierino Algieri
Keith O'Brien
N.W. Adventure Activities
Gwasg Carreg Gwalch

© publication: Gwasg Carreg Gwalch 2016

ISBN: 978-1-84524-251-0

Cover design: Eleri Owen
Cover image: Keith O'Brien

Published by Gwasg Carreg Gwalch,
12 Iard yr Orsaf, Llanrwst, Wales LL26 0EH
tel: 01492 642031
email: llanrwst@carreg-gwalch.com
website: www.carreg-gwalch.com

Capel y Ffin (capel: *'chapel'*; y ffin: *'the border'*)

Contents

Foreword

Some are short, clean, minimal and just do the job. Some are windbags. Some are geographical, historical or biblical. Some are still sore from the memory of a pit tragedy or a drowned valley. Some are lyrical and poetic. Some are musical; some are majestic. Some are very similar and some are very strange. But they are all our place names and they are very special, as are the places where they are rooted. They are distinctive and peculiar – and all are pronounceable!

Most of the elements in these names are Welsh, of course. But some Latin touches shows that the legacy of the Roman Empire extends to more than just road-making. A few Viking and Irish names along the Welsh coast tell the story of old strongholds of these maritime adventurers and invaders. Norman French names have stood the test of time in the shadow of their stone castles. English names, and English misspelt corruptions of the vernacular, still exist although many have been corrected by now and the old 'conqueror draws up the maps and names the places' ethic has dwindled. Using different languages and respect their qualities should not scare us.

A Welsh speaker reads out aloud Italian words from the menu in a Sicilian restaurant in the English border town of Chester. 'A! You speak Italian,' says the waiter with a sparkle and a wide smile. No, but Welsh and Italian are very similar when it comes to pronunciation. Both are phonetic: every letter is pronounced in the same way every time. Both places the stress on the penultimate syllable and both have nice open vowels. 'Ciao!' says the satisfied Welshman when he leaves. The waiter thanks him in Welsh, 'Diolch yn fawr!' Languages are not barriers, they are bridges.

A young man from Tokyo in Japan, Takeshi Koike, came to a university in Wales to learn English. He heard Welsh in the town and was interested. Later, he switched courses – because he found Welsh easier. He now runs Welsh learning classes in Japan and has sixty students. With a little effort, borders melt away.

In the 1960s and 1970s there was a strong movement to restore pride and respect to the Welsh language, especially in its use in public places, strengthening its status and equality. The road signs' campaign started as mass public law-breaking – people openly painting over English place names with bright green paint. Arrests led to court hearings, fines and jail sentences. Switching to more undercover tactics, the campaigners started painting by night. The whole of Wales was painted green. Still the authorities refused to allow Welsh place names on the signs with the usual excuses – too costly, too dangerous. The daubing stopped and removing road signs with bolt-cutters started. This was more serious stuff – there were cases of theft of government property and the leaders of Cymdeithas yr Iaith Gymraeg had a crown court hearing on a conspiracy charge. Mass rallies and the ritual display of stolen and damaged road signs kept the campaign in the headlines and in the end the government yielded to popular demand. But not before the British state had handed out criminal records to many who held the view that Welsh place names were important gateways to our culture.

The political campaign for Welsh road signs was more than a superficial campaign to wrestle power from the central offices of London. It is true that the owner of the name owns the territory, but the actual words in question struck at the core of the population. Welsh people just love their place names. They carve them on slates, create displays of them in wrought iron and embroider them on rugby shirts. They write poetry about them and include them in rhythmic metres. Place names sing in Wales. Children learn word craft by changing lists of place names into verse.

The meaning and origin of place names is a favourite national Welsh sport. People discuss them daily and university professors lecture on them. Radio and television create programmes about them and a library of books have been published on the topic. This interest follows them to other lands. A Welsh speaker will recognise Perth and Glasgow in Scotland as relatives to the words *perth* (hedge) and *glasgoed* (green wood) that he uses. In England, Dover is recognised of the same origin as *dyfroedd* (waters) and Devon of the same origin as *dyfnant* (deep valley). In Cornwall, a Welsh speaker has a whale of a time for he can recognise nearly all the elements, even if some of them are still corrupted in their spelling.

No doubt, these give Wales a flavour which is completely different to what is seen over the border in England. Many travellers wonder where all these names come from and what do they mean. This book is a helping hand to the bewildered stranger but is also of interest to the Welsh, who have taken these names for granted since childhood. They are tied into our history and heritage and open avenues into the Welsh language and its literature. If you understand a few place names, you are on your way to be a Welsh speaker!

A Little History

The Welsh language is directly descended from the Celtic language of ancient Gaul and pre-Roman Britain. The root form of the language – Brythonic Celtic – has been spoken here for three thousand years. Around AD 450, after the Romans left Celtic Britain, the Brythonic evolved to give us Early Welsh. What the Latin is to Italian, Brythonic is to Welsh – one could call it Ancient Welsh, in the same way as we say 'Ancient Greek'. Its closest relatives are Cornish and Breton and it has a kinship and close links as well with Irish, Scottish and Manx Gaelic.

Celtic style round houses, Felin Uchaf, Llŷn

Secrets

Every landscape treasures its secrets. Children stumble across them without any immediate need to put them into words. Beyond the narrow belt of trees, above the sheep droppings and the clumps of gorse and limestone outcrops, there is a cave on the hillside that is equally suitable for prehistoric man, bandits, Indians, and schoolboys smoking their first cigarette. The school textbook says that in one 'chamber' of the cave fifteen skeletons were found closely packed together in a crouched position. A delectable, mute, mystery. And on top of the hill, the man-made tumulus is named Y Gop, where local legend persists in saying Boadicea is buried. A long way from home. What language did she speak? Dig our soil and you find eloquent oval cups, oak overlaid with gold, and thin breastplates for horses embossed and worked by hands that knew how to speak without words. The views from the hilltop are enticing, intoxicating. North-east lies the Wirral, where the Green Knight hides, mixing Celtic legends with Middle-English poetry. Westwards the white strength of Gwynedd, and the mountains rising like ramparts to touch the setting sun. From every point of the compass this unique landscape hides treasure trove. Even the impassive vastness of the level sea conceals sunken cities with secret histories, myths and legends.

To each mystery there must be a key: but the key of keys is the original language which hallows every hill and valley, every farm and every field with its own revered name. I must learn it and the more difficult it is the better. Hidden treasures like pearls and lost souls need to have their price. Cromlechs and chronicles, Celtic crosses and Roman mines, castles and chapels, wells, caves, coalmines and churches, ruined abbeys and choirs, 'the woods, waters, meadows, combes, vales/All the air things wear that build this world of Wales'.[1]

Emyr Humphreys from *Discovering Welshness* (1992)

Moel Hebog sunset

Why is Pronunciation Important?

If you're a visitor to Wales or you've recently come to live here, and you need to ask the way to somewhere, it can be a bit of a challenge. It's fine if you want to go to a place with a straightforward short name like Bangor or Corwen, but if you're heading for Rhosllannerchrugog, Llwyngwril or Llanrhaeadr-ym-Mochant, you may be tempted to admit defeat and just point at the mind-bending string of letters in the guidebook.

It would be very satisfying, wouldn't it, to be able to reel off Troedrhiwdalar or Pontrhydfendigaid as easily as Birmingham or Newcastle? But most people are put off from even trying because they get the impression that the pronunciation of names like these must be very difficult, or even impossible, if you're not Welsh. They look at Betws-

y-coed, for example, and can't work out what to do with the '*w*', so they just leave it out and end up, as often as not, with that well-known Welsh schoolgirl, Betsy Co-Ed. Some of the Welsh used to believe they had longer tongues than the English, so they could pronounce words that the English couldn't, and when you're faced with something like Eglwyswrw or Llanuwchllyn, you could be forgiven for thinking they might have been right.

So let's get one thing clear straight away. The idea that Welsh pronunciation is difficult is *complete nonsense*.

Welsh spelling, unlike English spelling, is extremely tidy and regular and the rules are mostly very simple and logical. Once you know the rules, you can pronounce almost any Welsh word correctly on sight. And most of the sounds you find in Welsh are the same, or as near as makes no difference, as sounds we have in English.

Take our old friend Betws-y-coed. The trick here is to know that the '*w*' is pronounced like an English 'oo'. If you say bettooss a koid, sounding it just as if it was a string of English words, then you'll have almost exactly the correct Welsh pronunciation. There's nothing there that needs a longer than average tongue, and there's nothing there that breaks the standard Welsh spelling rules.

It's true, of course, that there are a few difficult sounds in Welsh names – the famous '*ll*', for example – but there's no law that says you have to get them 100% right. People who weren't brought up to speak English often have trouble with 'th' and say things like 'What eezzeess?' for 'What is this?', but that doesn't stop English people from understanding them.

So why not have a go? You never know, you might surprise yourself next time you're doing a commentary on your holiday video of Penrhyndeudraeth.[2]

A Little Grammar

A few casual glances show that Welsh is quite different to English. The words are unfamiliar but once a few simple words are learnt – e.g. *bach* (small), *mawr* (big) – you will notice that the word pattern is also completely different to English. The word for mountain is *mynydd* and therefore an English monoglot would expect Big Mountain to be displayed as *Mawr Mynydd*, but it is the opposite order in Welsh – *Mynydd Mawr*. Welsh, like other languages from central and southern Europe, generally puts the adjective after the noun.

In the same way, where English says Hopkinston (Hopkin's town), Welsh says Trehopcyn (*tre* being Welsh for town). Other describing nouns such as *traeth* (beach), *bryn* (hill), *aber* (estuary) follow this pattern. Another pattern is Pen-y-nant (*pen*: top/summit/head; *nant*: valley/glen/brook). The literal translation is 'the head of the valley', but '*y*' (the) is sufficient in Welsh, the word 'of' is not needed.

In the study of place names, we realise quite early on that there are different versions of words on the signposts. As in other European languages, there are two forms of some adjectives in Welsh – masculine and feminine:

gwyn/gwen (white)

Welsh, also like other languages, has kept its plural adjectives in some cases:

du/duon (black)

First letters vary as well and we have different versions of:

bach/fach (small)

mawr/fawr (big; large)
poeth/boeth (hot)
gwyllt/wyllt (wild)

This phenomenon is known as 'mutation'. It occurs in English as well, but not in the same way. It's the smoothing of letters on the tongue to create fluidity of speech. Such mutations, however, can make tracing words through a dictionary a little problematic for the newcomer.

Pronunciation Guides

Being a phonetic language, Welsh letters adhere usually to a single way of pronunciation:

c – k (hard)
ch – as in loch
dd – th as in that
f – v
ff – f
g – g (hard)
ll – pronounce l, keep tongue in position at roof of mouth, and breathe out!
the – th as in think

There are 7 vowels, a, e, i, o, u, w and y. Pronunciation may be long or short.

w may be as in pool, or pull e.g. *cwm* (coom) – valley
y may be as in fun, or pin e.g. *y, yr* (u, ur) – the, *dyffryn* (dufrin) – valley.

A Challenge

To get you off to a flying start, why not grasp the nettle and have a go at

The Notorious Welsh 'LL'

It's not nearly as hard as people imagine, and if you can get it right, it will make your Welsh pronunciation sound really impressive. And if you can't, so what? You can easily fudge it.

So here goes:

* put the TIP of your TONGUE against the back of your TOP TEETH, just where they meet the gum. (The TTTT rule.)
* Hold it in that position.
* Blow gently.

And that's it.

Practice it a few times, then see if you can manage to slip it into a few Welsh words like:

Llandeilo
Llandrindod
Llangollen
Llanelli

Remember 'll' has this sound anywhere in a Welsh word, not just at the beginning.
   Can't do it? Never mind. Just say 'thl' instead.[2]

Llangollen steam railway

The 'Meaning' of Place Names

The Welsh would sooner ask 'Where do you come from?' rather than 'What do you do?' They will not rest until they have a street or a village name. Yes, we are nosey by nature, but this question stems from our deep interest in roots. Place names are more than a collection of consonants and vowels. They are more than road directions, more than just pronunciations. They are signposts to the past, firmly planted in the present. They link our today to all our yesterdays and are symbols of the continuity of society in its own environment. They help us to reclaim the meaningful past and to set foundations for a continuing future.

Place names are an integral part of the world in which we live, be they names of towns and villages, names of features in the landscape, or names of streets and houses. We describe our environment by the names which we give to its features and thus we are able to recognise our communities which we share together. The names may be strictly descriptive topographically – the meeting place of two streams, the nature of the terrain, some outstanding feature; they may be facetious, or denote ownership or usage, but they all had, at the time of naming, some significance.

Place names have meaning beyond the dictionary definitions of their elements. Place names have, for that reason, been called 'signposts to the past' because discovering their deeper significance can tell us so much about a variety of topics – farming practices, enclosures, the coming of industrialisation, boundaries, ownership and tenancies, changes in the environment, the nature of society. Places are named in the language of the community and thus they are able to speak to us across the centuries of changes in that language and its dialects.[3]

Brynley F. Roberts

A protest by a language movement

A Direction to our Past

Place names preserve folk memory and ancient 'forgotten' facts, as the academic broadcaster Bedwyr Lewis Jones discovered when he enjoyed the company of cultured members of different communities on his lecturing travels across the county:

I remember well his delight in discovering fragments of real antiquity in the everyday language of people. Such discoveries depended, to a large degree, on his own knowledge of the past, a knowledge which provided him with a context that those using old expressions or words did not know. He was very excited – and excitement about

discoveries and new insights were of the essence of his learning and knowledge – when he heard someone in Powys refer to the sharp east wind there as 'wind from the old Pengwern'. He immediately recognized Pengwern as the old Welsh name for the region around modern Shrewsbury, and the name of an ancient Welsh court in that area. The memory of the old Pengwern had survived in Powys, in the speech of some of its people, for centuries. He was equally excited when he heard someone in his native Anglesey refer to the social services department in the county in this way, 'Caiff Berffro dalu' ('Berffro can pay'). He realized that deep in the consciousness or, maybe, in the subconscious of his speaker was the feeling that the centre of some kind of government in Anglesey was not Llangefni, but Aberffraw, the seat of the ancient Welsh princes. The memory of the medieval Welsh court had lodged itself in the speech of some of the people of Anglesey until the 20th century. Such debris retained in the living language, spoken by people in their patch for hundreds of years, fascinated him. We are now at a stage when this kind of richness retained in the continuity of a language is coming to an end – in English and Welsh. The ease of movement of people from one place to another, and the overwhelming influence of the media erased such riches from our speech. Bedwyr would have been delighted with the excavation of an old Welsh court at Rhosyr, just outside Niwbwrch, in a field which had always been known to the locals as Cae Llys (*court field*)!

It is important that Bedwyr's study of place names is now translated into English, because such a study requires the attention of an expert, and the study of place names seems to draw to it the consideration of many persons who are anything but experts. This is an authoritative as well as a most entertaining study, and one that will reveal to the reader Bedwyr's unique and warm personality.[5]

Gwyn Thomas

Rhosyr, Môn – the site of a Welsh court

The Name of the Country

Cymru is the name of our country in Welsh, but *Wales* in English. Both names have an interesting history.

Wales to begin with. That goes back ultimately to a word *walh* or *wealh* meaning 'foreign, foreigner' in Germanic, the early language from which sprang English and German. *Walh* was the word used by Germanic speakers on the continent around 2,000 years ago for a person whose language they didn't understand.

Thus *walh* was used of anyone speaking Latin. That is why *Walloon* is the present-day name for those people in Belgium who speak French, which is a late form of Latin. The meaning of *wall* at the beginning of the name is 'foreign', since in the eyes of the early Germanic people the Latin of the *Belgae* was a foreign language.

Britain was full of people speaking in foreign tongues – some in Latin and a great many more in Brythonic, a Celtic tongue. The whole lot were *walh*, 'foreign', or – in the plural – *wealas*, 'foreigners'. 'Welsh' and 'Wales' are much later forms of *wealas*. In the eyes of the early English, we – the Welsh – were foreigners, even in our own country!

The same thing was true as regards the people of Cornwall. *Cornwealas* was the English name for them – i.e. the *wealas* or foreigners who lived in the 'Horn of land' or peninsula. Later on *Cornwealas* changed to *Cornwall*.

The *wall* at the end of *Cornwall* is the same word at root as the *wal* at the beginning of *Wales* and the *wall* at the beginning of *Walloon*. It is also identical with the *wal* in *walnut* – a nut that was *foreign* to Britain.

The source of *Cymry*, our own name for ourselves, is completely different. *Cymry* is the plural of *Cymro*; and *Cymro* goes back to a word in very early Welsh – and before that in Brythonic – which was a combination of *com* and *bro*, the latter word meaning 'region, territory within a boundary'. The original meaning of the name *Cymro* was 'a man from the same region, a man from a country or district within a boundary'. So the meaning of *Cymry* is 'people from the same country, compatriots'.

Offa's Dyke, Radnorshire

At one time a *b* came after the *m* in the name, but *mb* changed to *m* by around the year 600. The *mb* has remained in the Latin form *Cambria*, and from the Latin *Cambria* comes *Cambrian* in English – a term which is used, for example, to denote very ancient rocks.

The *mb* also survives in the names *Cumbria* and *Cumberland* in the north of England. These names are forms of *Cymry*. Long ago Cumberland was a land of the *Cymry*, before the *Cymry* there were conquered by the English. At that time the people of Cumbria and those of our own Wales saw themselves as compatriots. We too continue to call the north of England and the south of Scotland 'the Old North' – *our* Old North.[5]

The 'Welsh' Element in Britain

To some people, the claim that place names which are essentially 'Welsh' in character are to be found almost everywhere in Scotland and England might come as a surprise and can be met by a certain amount of disbelief. This stems from ignoring the fact that the original term 'British' derives from 'Brythonic' – the Celtic group of tribes which inhabited southern Britain up to the Clyde and Forth rivers during the pre-Roman Iron Age. (These were also referred to by English historians as 'Ancient Britons' at one time.)

The description *British Isles* first appeared in historical records somewhere around 400 BC and applied to all the islands in the group including the two that are now known as 'Great Britain' and 'Ireland'. When the Romans arrived in this island some 2,000 years ago they called the inhabitants 'British', but when the Angles and Saxons came some half a millennium later they called *the very same people* 'Welsh'! Thereafter the terms 'British' or 'Welsh' were synonymous and were used interchangeably until, in the year 1707, the Parliaments of England and Scotland were united to form the first Parliament of 'Great Britain'. Overnight the term *British* changed from its original meaning and came to mean a 'Citizen of Great Britain'; later still it changed again and nowadays it is understood to mean a 'Citizen of the United Kingdom of Great Britain & Northern Ireland'. Thus place names, found anywhere in England, Scotland or Wales, which survive from Roman or pre-Roman times and have their roots in the Brythonic language can legitimately be referred to as 'Brythonic' in its original sense of it being the language of the Britons during those early years. Unfortunately, very few people today will claim to have a subjective understanding or clear comprehension of anything described as *Brythonic*, yet they can immediately understand and relate to a language described as 'very early Welsh' – which is exactly what Brythonic was. That is why language

The Welsh stronghold of Dolwyddelan

descriptions such as *British*, *Brythonic*, *Cumbric*, *Cymric* or *Pictish* will, although pedantically correct, be avoided wherever possible in favour of the simpler and more universally understood description *Welsh*.[8]

Among the Brythonic tribes in Celtic Britain, the Ordovices (north-western), Deceangli (north-eastern), Demetae (south-western), Silures (south-eastern) and the Cornovii (Powys/north-central) held lands in the country now known as Wales. Brythonic speech absorbed a number of Latin words during the Roman occupation and after the departure of the legions, 'old Welsh' was evolved from the unwritten Brythonic tongue around 450.

The emergence of Old Welsh coincided with the raids of Saxon pirates in south-eastern Britain, raids which led to occupation and wars with the Brythonic people.

The Anglo-Saxons, of course, were a Germanic people whose language – now usually referred to as Old English – was closely related to the Old Norse spoken by the Vikings who came later. In Anglo-Saxon eyes the British were a foreign people – a view reflected in the Old English term *walas*, 'foreigners', used to describe them.[7]

Old Welsh lost ground to the east, but in the mountains of the west, found a stronghold.

Welsh as a distinct language emerged out of these marginalised beginnings and established itself within 'Wales' by the oral commonplace of everyday speech. It was the language of the common people and also of sage, poet, academic and magician. Welsh flourished with its Celtic embroidery of words used to narrate the Early Welsh Stories, those fabulous accounts of mystery, myth, tradition and legends. Welsh, written down, formed one of the earliest records of writing in what was otherwise an almost illiterate Europe.[9]

Through the centuries, the language underwent construction and vocabulary

South-eastern castles: 1. Cardiff; 2. Whitecastle

changes as it survived invasions by Saxon, Viking, Irish, Norman and English. Then, in 1588, there appeared a momentous publication: a translation of the Holy Bible into Welsh by Bishop William Morgan (who was born in 1541 at a house called Tŷ Mawr in the hills above Penmachno). The Welsh Bible became at once a monumental literary resource not only for Welsh academics, bishops and poets but for the common Welshman and his family to learn to read. Bishop Morgan's Bible provided, by the outstanding accomplishment and quality of its linguistic excellence, a standard written form of the Welsh language, the very best in Welsh vocabulary and idiom of Welsh expression. It is the rock on which the present Welsh language is so strongly built. It marks the sudden appearance of a cohesive standard language, Modern Welsh. Its publication, without a shadow of doubt, saved the Welsh language from degeneration and decay as Welsh weakened in the Celtic twilight with successive and recent invasions and incursions by the English.[9]

The presence of an empire-building next door neighbour was to cast its shadow, of course. This empire was now called 'British', but it had no connection with the early Celtic definition of that term.

Wales became overrun and ruled by the English. The 1536 Act of Union, in one outrageously insensitive surgical act without anaesthetic, 'incorporated, united and annexed' Wales to England. Economic and political coercion by the English, from the early 16th century onward, attempted to deliberately stamp out the Welsh language completely (the English succeeded in rooting out Irish, except in patches in places in the west and the remote western islands, the Irish-speaking areas, An Ghaeltacht).

Welsh was openly derided and prohibited as a medium for education and office in public life. The Education Act of 1870 made English the only language of instruction in Welsh schools and outlawed the use of Welsh in a child's education. A crude but effective punishment to stop Welsh children using their own language in class or in the playground was the enforced wearing of a token called the Welsh Not (a placard hung around the neck), passed on from culprit to culprit until, at the end of the school day for whoever was last to possess it, a thrashing, a caning. Welsh was the first and only language of these children at home. The Welsh language was under great threat of complete loss by such systematic eradication.[9]

As the language became marginalised to chapel and hearth in its own country, all official work – including the use of place names – was done in English, for the English state.

Britishness is a political ideology, as is Communism. It isn't a nation. As the philosopher J. R. Jones said in 1966 in his book, *Prydeindod*, 'There already exists such a thing as a British nationality; it is the English one.'

The 'British nation', likewise, is not a nation as it does not have a *priod iaith* (indigenous language). There is no 'British language'. It is not Switzerland, where a new nationality has been agreed, with the constituent *priod iaith* being recognised and respected as an organic part of that state. The British nationality is an extension of English nationality. Its *priod iaith* is English – as the name suggests, it is the language of the English people and state.[10]

Welsh, as a living language, has survived, however. Since 2011, it is one of the official languages of Wales – equal in status, legality and rights. It is even more present on the streets and roads of the country and its place names have been preserved to be understood and enjoyed.

The Latin Element

The Roman era began in Wales with a military invasion in AD 48 and ended when the country was abandoned in AD 383. Wales was a rich source of mineral wealth and apart from extracting large amounts of gold, copper, lead, zinc and silver from these rocks, the occupation was mainly a military one. The only part of Wales to be Romanised was the extreme south-eastern corner and the Gower peninsula.

Caerwent was the only town founded by the Romans in Wales and its original character is very visible there today. Aside from the Roman lifestyle remains along the southern coast, the main archaeological remains in Wales are military roads and fortifications. The Romans, however, did leave traces of Latin in present-day place names.

The Welsh name *stryd* (street) derives from the Latin *strata* and the prefix *caer* (fort) usually signifies that a Roman fort (*castra*) was at that site. The Romans were great bridge builders when creating their roadworks and the Welsh word *pont* (bridge) derives from Latin.

Sarn Elen

This name is given to Roman roads throughout Wales. According to legend, Elen of Wales (a princess who lived in a castle in Caernarfon) was the wife of Emperor Magnus Maximus and mother of Constantine. Traditionally, she was responsible for the Roman roads that were built across the country: *Sarn Elen* (the road of Elen). There is also a suggestion that the original form was *sarn halen* (salt road).

Roman remains at Caer-went

Welsh and English

After the Anglo-Saxons arrived in eastern Britain (from the 5th and 6th century onwards), many place names from both sides of the border derive from neighbouring influences.

Many rivers in England are called Avon which is the Welsh word (spelt *afon*) for river! The Welsh for lake (*llyn*) is the root of both King's Lynn and Lincoln. Malvern is *moel* (barren) *fryn* (hill); Long Mynd is *mynydd* (mountain) and Ince is *ynys* (island).

On the western side of the border, place names ending in *cot* (cottage), *den* (valley), *ey* (island) and *ton* (farm/township) are the visual remains of Anglo-Saxon influence.

*The second Severn crossing
– the river is called Afon Hafren*

Viking Voices

The Vikings from Denmark and Norway attacked the shores of Wales from 798 onwards. They established colonies in Dublin, Waterford and the Isle of Man, and the Welsh coast was within convenient raiding distance for their long boats.

Initial plundering developed to colonisation with small Viking villages being set up along the coastline. With the occupation came the place names.

Anglesey   A Viking called *Ongull* gave his name to the island (island was also called *–ey* by the Vikings)

Bardsey   Named after a Viking called *Barthr*

The sacred island of Bardsey (above)
Llanddwyn on the western shore of Anglesey (opposite)

Caldey   *Kald* means cold

Swansea   A thousand years ago the people living along the coast of Wales were well aware of the men of Scandinavia – the Vikings. They were a plague to coastal folk, sailing in their sharp-prowed ships from their kingdoms around Dublin and in the northern isles of Scotland, making attacks on inhabited centres, plundering monasteries and churches, and snatching locals to sell as slaves.

It was some of these Vikings who named the mouth of the river Tawe 'Sveinn's island' after one of their leaders. At that time the course of the river near its mouth was very different from what it is today. Some sort of island existed there, and the river forked around it.

When the Normans came to the area sometime towards 1100 or soon afterwards and built a town and a castle, they could have adopted the – geographical – Welsh name Abertawe ('mouth of the Tawe'). But they didn't do so. Instead they accepted the Scandinavian name and, in the course of time, that turned into *Swansea*.

Holm   Another Viking name for 'small island' as in Flat Holm, Priestholm.

Skar, sker, stack A rock in the seas in Blackscar, Skerries, South Stack.

South Stack island and lighthouse in the distance, from North Stack (Ynys Lawd and Ynys Arw in Welsh)

Norman Names

The Norman conquest of England in 1066 saw the start of two hundred years of Norman wars in Wales. Greedy barons were resisted by resilient Welsh princes, and regions and castles were attacked and changed hands many times during those turbulent years. Norman French elements can still be traced in some Welsh place names, especially in the shadows of the Norman castles.

Montgomery	Named after the Norman lord of the castle, Roger de Montgomery, who took his name from his castle in Normandy: Montgommery
Beaumaris	*beau* (beautiful) *marais* (alder swamp)
Mold	*mont* (hill) *hault* (high)
Grosmont	*gros* (big) *mont* (hill)
Grace Dieu	'the grace of God'
Rockfield	named after Rocheville in Normandy

Montgomery castle, Powys

Land of the Bible

Bethlehem, Ebeneser, Bethesda

It's a very unexpected thing for visitors from a foreign country to see *Bethlehem* and *Nasareth* on names on road signs here in Wales.

Bethlehem is a village in the parish of Llangadog in Carmarthenshire. It's a small place – only a few houses, a post office and an Independent chapel. It's the post office which has made it famous during the course of recent years. Ever since special stamps began to be issued in celebration of Christmas, hundreds of people have been posting their Christmas cards in the village so as to get the *Bethlehem* postmark on them.

The village got its name from the Independent chapel, which was built there around 1820 and called *Bethlehem*.

The same thing happened in the case of *Nasareth*, near Llanllyfni in Arfon. The Independent chapel there was built in 1823. In 1867, as the population increased following the growth of the slate industry, another chapel was built. This was called *Nasareth*, which also became the name for the houses around it.

Similar place names occur in many places in Wales.

Bethesda is a former slate-quarrying village on the A5 near Bangor. It grew around the Independent chapel, built in 1820, from which it took its name. The Penrhyn quarries, which are such a prominent feature of the landscape hereabouts, were first developed by Richard Pennant around 1765, and by 1875 they were the largest in the world, employing more than 2,000 workers. The Penrhyn Lockouts of 1896–7 and 1900–3 were one of the most serious disputes in the history of Welsh industry. At the heart of the confrontation between the men and the owner was the right to belong to a union and the way in which wages were fixed by management. The community suffered grievous

Soar – a chapel which gives its name to the rural Soar y Mynydd in Ceredigion

damage as a result of the owners' intransigence, with many people leaving the district in search of work elsewhere. There were great cultural differences between the quarry owners (Anglicized and Church of England) and the quarrymen (Welsh and nonconformists).[5]

Lists of Place Names

In the following lists, which have been sorted into different groups of place names, there are Welsh words commonly found across the country and also specific place names with more information, history and narrative to them.

*Llyn Padarn, Snowdonia
with low clouds*

Adjectives

arian	silver	*arry-ann*
aur	gold	*ire*
bach (fach)	small	*bahk* ('ah' as in 'ah!')
Felin-fach	*melin* (mill) mutates and the adjective *bach* following it also mutates.	
brith (frith)	mottled	*breeth*
Brithdir	*tir* (land) mutates and the name indicates 'land composed of soils or vegetation of different colours' or 'land dotted with stones'. Common throughout Wales.	
bychan (fychan/fechan)	little	*buckann*
byr (fyr/fer)	short	*beer*
caled (galed)	hard	*kalledd*
cam (gam)	crooked	*kamm*
canol (ganol)	middle	*kannoll*
clyd	sheltered	*kleed*
coch (goch)	red	*kawk*
Castell Coch	(red castle) common in many places and usually built with red sandstone.	
crin (grin)	withered	*krinn*
crwn (grwn/gron)	round	*kroon*
diffaith (ddiffaith)	barren	*deefeyth*
Garndiffaith	*carn* (cairn or hill) which is desolate or wild and barren.	
du (ddu)	black	*dee*

Castell Coch, near Cardiff

Dulas	name of a river, very common in Wales. The second element is *glais* (stream) not *glas* (blue) as seen in Aberdulais.	
duon	black (plural)	*deeonn*
Cerrig Duon	*cerrig* is the plural of *carreg* and *duon* is the plural of *du*, 'black, dark'. A prehistoric circle of stones.[6]	
dyrys (ddyrys)	difficult	*durriss*
garw (arw)	rough	*garroo*
glas (las)	blue	*glahss* ('ah' as in 'ah!')
Bryn Glas	site of a famous Welsh victory in Radnorshire in the summer of 1402 during the Revolt of Owain Glyndŵr and a common name – *bryn* (hill) *glas* (green/verdant)	
gwen (wen)	white, fair	*gwenn*
gwyn (wyn)	white, fair	*gwinn*
hen	old	*hane*
Hengoed	*coed* (wood or trees); therefore 'old wood or trees'	
heulog	sunny	*hailogg*
hir	long	*here*
Hirnant	*nant* means 'valley' as in Nant Ffrancon and Nant Peris (Gwynedd); 'long valley'	
hyfryd	pleasant	*huvv-ridd*
is	lower	*eess*
isa (isaf)	lowest	*issavv*
llwyd (lwyd)	grey	*thlooidd*
llydan (lydan)	wide	*thluddann*
Gorslydan	*gors* (bog, fen); therefore wide or broad swamp	
mawr (fawr)	big, large	*mowr* ('mow' rhymes with 'now')
Bryn-mawr	an industrial town in Gwent, established around Bryn-mawr farm *c.*1800; *bryn* (hill), *mawr* (big)	

Tŷ Mawr Wybrnant	*tŷ* (house). Tŷ Mawr is a remotely situated old farmhouse in Gwybrnant on a minor road above Penmachno. It was the birthplace of William Morgan (1545–1604), the first translator of the Bible into Welsh. Now restored and open to visitors during the summer months, the house has a small exhibition illustrating the life and work of the great man.	
melyn (felyn/felen)	yellow	*mellinn*
melys (felys)	sweet	*melliss*
moel (foel)	bare hilltop	*moil*
mwyn (fwyn)	mild, ore	*mooinn*
newydd	new	*naywith*
Capel Newydd	*capel* (chapel); there is an example on the mountain between Llanofer and Blaenafon (Gwent), standing till *c*.1861.	
oer	cold	*oir*
Cwm-ffrwd-oer (south-eastern Wales)	*cwm* (valley); *ffrwd* (stream/brook) – 'valley of the cold stream'	
poeth (boeth)	hot	*poith*
Pentre-poeth	*pentref* (village). *Poeth* in the sense of 'burnt' probably, or it might refer to the burning of charcoal for local industry.	
sych	dry	*seek*
Sycharth	*arth* (enclosed area). Sycharth is a dry mount close to the border with England near Llansilin. Here, Owain Glyndŵr (*c*.1354–1416), the national hero of the Welsh, had a manor until he rose in revolt against the English Crown in 1400. The poet Iolo Goch (*c*.1325–*c*.1398), writing in the 1380s, drew an idyllic picture of life at Sycharth.	
tawel (dawel)	calm	*towell* ('tow' rhymes with 'now')

Sycharth

teg (**deg**)	fair	*taigg*
Pant-teg (Panteg)	'The fair hollow'	
tywyll (**dywyll**)	dark	*towill* ('tow' and *ll* – see page 16)
ucha (**uchaf**)	highest	*ickah*
ystwyth	winding	*uss-tooith*

Prepositions and Positions

Place names can be simply very specific in Welsh. The names themselves are often actual directions – 'under the rock', 'at the head of the valley', 'by the brook'.

ar	on	*arr*
Argoed	*coed* (woodland/trees), for a place 'near to or facing a wood'. Common throughout Wales.[6]	
blaen (flaen)	summit/head	*bline*
Blaen-y-cwm	*cwm* (valley). Usually a farm at 'the headwaters of the valley'.	
cil (gil)	corner	*kill*
Cilmeri	*meri*, probably compressed from *mieri* (brambles) – a remote or hidden place behind brambles. At Cilmeri (Breconshire) stands the stone of Llywelyn ap Gruffudd, the prince of Wales who lead the second War of Independence against the Normans. He was killed nearby on 11 December 1282.	
dan (tan)	under	*dann*
Dan yr Ogof	*yr ogof* (the cave). This is the site of spectacular underground caverns in carboniferous limestone in the Brecon Beacons and originates with the former farm just below the cave given as Ogof yr Esgyrn, 'the cave of the bones'.	
ger	near	*gerr*
is	under/below	*eess*

Cilmeri

pen (**ben**)	top/head	*penn*
Pennant	*nant* (valley) meaning 'upper reaches, top of the valley'. Very common.	
Penderyn	A famous Welsh whisky, *deryn* (bird). Earlier forms include the definite article *y*: *Pen y deryn*.	

The original meaning was *bird's head*, or *the bird's head*. It was totemistic in nature, marking a boundary line or a meeting place, with religious and tribal significances.

tal	end/head	*tal* (rhymes with 'pal')
Tal-y-bont	*y bont* (the bridge). *Pont* mutated after the definite article gives us a place name of a 'village at the end of a bridge'. Common throughout the country.	
Tal-y-fan	*y fan* (the peak). A name on quite a few summits (e.g. in the Conwy Valley and near Builth): 'end of the peak'.	
Tal-y-llyn	*y llyn* (the lake) as in Tal-y-llyn (Meirionnydd) and Llangasty Tal-y-llyn (Llyn Syfaddan/Llan-gors Lake).	
tan (**dan**)	under	*tann*
traws (**draws**)	across	*trowss* (rhymes with 'grouse')
Trawsgoed	*goed*, mutated (wood/trees) – 'over, across' and 'wood' with the general sense of 'an area covered by wood'.	
Trawsfynydd	*mynydd*, mutated (mountain) – 'across the mountain'. A village in Meirionnydd, off A470. A bronze statue in the village commemorates the young poet Ellis Humphrey Evans (Hedd Wyn; 1887–1917), portrayed as a shepherd, who was brought up at the nearby farm known as Yr Ysgwrn, now a museum.	

Hedd Wyn worked for his father before enlisting with the Royal Welch Fusiliers during the First World War and was killed in action at Pilkem Ridge in July 1917. He was

posthumously awarded the Chair at the National Eisteddfod held in Birkenhead in the following September. The announcement of his death was received with great emotion by the audience and during the chairing ceremony the empty chair was draped in black. The place name Trawsfynydd and its undertones are powerfully included in an elegy composed to him by master-poet R. Williams Parry.

Uwchlaw'r Ffynnon

name of a farm in Gwynedd which is situated above the parish saint's *ffynnon* (well)

Hills and Mountains

ban	peak	*bann*
bar	head/summit	*barr*
Berwyn	these hills in central Wales probably derive from *bar* (head/summit) and *gwyn*, mutated, (white)	
blaen	summit/head	*bline*
blaenau	summits	*bline-eye*
blaidd	wolf	*blithe*
boncyn	hillock	*bonn-kinn*
bron (fron)	slope	*bronn*
brwyn	rushes	*bruinn*
bugail	shepherd	*biggile* (rhymes with 'smile')
bwlch	gap, pass	*boolk*
Bwlch y Ddeufaen	*y ddeufaen* ('the two stones'). In this pass above the Conwy valley there are two standing stones from prehistoric times.	
cadair (cader)	chair	*kaddire* (rhymes with 'fire')
carn	cairn	*karn*
carnedd	cairn	*karneth*
Carnedd Llywelyn	the second highest peak in Wales combines *carnedd* (heap, tumulus, mound) with the name of one of the princes of Wales, Llywelyn. Nearby stands another mountain commemorating another native prince, Carnedd Dafydd.	
carreg	stone	*karregg*
cefn	ridge	*kevvenn*
cerrig	stones	*kerrigg*

Cader Idris above Dolgellau

comins	common	*komm-ince*
corn	horn	*korn*
cors	bog	*korss*
craig (**graig**)	rock	*krye-g*
cribin	ridge	*kribbinn*
crug	hillock	*kreeg*

Yr Wyddgrug (Mold) Both names refer to the bailey hill in the top part of the town. Yr Wyddgrug means 'hill where there is a tumulus', i.e. *gŵydd* 'tumulus, burial ground' and *crug* 'hillock'. You will find Gwyddgrug in Carmarthenshire, and the elements are also to be seen in Crughywel (Crickhowell, Breconshire), Bryn-crug (Meirionnydd) and, of course, in Yr Wyddfa (Snowdon). Mold is a Norman name. The original form was probably *Mont-hault* 'high mountain', a name which developed in two directions. To the Normans and those who spoke French, it stayed similar to the forms you see in the second line above, before disappearing as an oral form. To the local inhabitants, *Mont-hault* developed in ordinary speech to give us the 'Mold' of today.

Cricieth *Crukeith*, spelt like that, is the earliest form found for the name *Cricieth*. It was recorded in 1273 or 1274, but the stone castle was one of the seats of the princes of Gwynedd since the 1230's.

Note that *u*, and not *i*, was the vowel in the first part. That tell us us that the word *crug*, meaning 'hillock', was the first element of the name – the same *crug* as in Crughywel (Crickhowell) and Crucadarn.

The second element was *ceith* or *caith* – a plural of *caeth*

Cricieth castle

and signifying 'bondmen' in English – either those who were tenants in bondage to the land and without rights, or possibly actual prison inmates. The *Chronicle of the Princes* tells us that Dafydd ap ('*son of*') Llywelyn Fawr ('the Great') imprisoned his brother 'in Cruceith': so the hillock or tump was the site of a prison.

In time *Cruceith* became *Crucieith*, with an *i* developing in speech after the *c* – ac in *ciapten* for *capten* ('captain'). Later on *Crucieith* became *Cricieith* – the *u* changing to *i* under the influence of the *i* sound that follows it. And then, by 1600, *Cricieith* became *Cricieth*.

In the case of Cricieth, the evidence of forms in old records makes it easy for us to trace how the name changed. But how to spell it? I've written one *c* in the middle of the name in this article, but some good people of the town say there ought to be two.

The truth is that down the centuries there have been around forty different ways of spelling the name. You find *c* and *k* for the first *c*; *c*, *kk*, *cc*, *ck* and even *kk* for the *c* in the middle; *t* as well as *th* for the *th* on the end; and other variations to denote the vowels.

This is not at all strange. Clerks, many of them foreign, had difficulty through the centuries in writing down Welsh names. And the standardisation of Welsh orthography was a comparatively late thing – i.e. the settling on an agreed standard way of spelling. That was brought about by Sir John Morris-Jones and his co-scholars around the beginning of the 19th century. It was agreed to write a single *c* and a single *m* at all times, even if – in strict phonetic terms – one or other of them was a double consonant. Thus it's Cricieth with one *c* which is correct. There's no arguing about that. The desire to write Criccieth is a whim, and nothing else.

Incidentally, it's the Welsh (or Brythonic) word *crug* which is found in the village name Crich near Derby, and in the second part of Penkridge between Stafford and Wolverhampton. At root, Penkridge represents *Pen-crug*.[5]

cyrn	horns	*keern*
drum	ridge	*drimm*
eira	snow	*airah* ('ah' rhymes with 'ah!')
eithin	gorse	*aithinn*
eryr	eagle	*erreer*
eryri	highlands	*err-yrree*

Eryri   the Welsh name for the highest mountain range in Wales, (Snowdonia in English). It's not 'the land of eagles' as generally misconceived, but it does share the same root. *Eryr* (eagle) is the highest flying bird; *Eryri* are the highest peaks.

esgair	ridge	*ess-kire* (rhymes with 'fire')
ffos	ditch	*fauss*
ffridd	pasture, alp	*freethe* (rhymes with 'breathe')

Ffrith   The word *ffrith* (or *ffridd* in parts of Wales) describes the area and it's often referred to as y *Ffrith* (the Ffrith). *Ffrith* has several meanings. The original meaning was 'woodland' and there are places in England such as Frith (Lancashire) and Chapel-en-le-Frith (Derbyshire). In Welsh additional meanings developed such as 'grazing land in the uplands or on the valley floor'; it can also refer to moor and heath. The most common meaning is probably 'land taken from the mountain'.[4]

gallt	hill/wooded slope	*gath-t*
garth	high enclosure	*garth*
gloddfa	quarry	*gloth-vah* ('ah' as in 'ah!')
gorsedd	seat/throne	*gorrseth*
Gorsedd		

Gorsedd is the name of a village near Whitford (or Chwitffordd) in Flintshire. It's also a word or element that occurs frequently in the names of fields and farms throughout Wales – *Penrorsedd* being one example.

Question people about the meaning of *gorsedd* and you get two answers. It means either (1) the throne of a king or queen, or (2) with a capital G, a society or special institution for poets. But these meanings of the word are comparatively late. It's hard to trace *gorsedd* in the sense of 'throne' further back than the 15th century – some 500 years ago. As for *Gorsedd* as an institution for poets, the word in that sense is over 200 years old. It was first used by Iolo Morganwg around 1791 for the meetings of poets he'd begun holding.

The word itself is much older, going back to the beginnings of Welsh and further still than that. One of the meanings of the word in its ancient usage was 'court' or 'assembly'. It occurs in the sense 'court of judgment' in the Laws of Hywel Dda. Another of its meanings was 'heap of earth', 'cairn', 'hillock' – frequently a hillock where there was a burial place or *tumulus*. (Witness the Gorsedd Arberth of the *Mabinogi*, a hill with 'sacred' connotations, full of mystery.)

There's a connection between these different meanings, once we bear in mind that it was customary to hold courts

Gorsedd meeting at Caerfyrddin (Carmarthen)

on hillocks in the open air – often on hillocks with 'sacred' associations.

In the Gorsedd near Whitford, the meaning is 'hill'; and an ancient grave or tumulus is also situated there. 'Hill' is the meaning too in the name *Yr Orsedd Goch* near Wrecsam (Wrexham) – a name that was Anglicized to give the present-day *Rossett*.

gwryd	fathom	*goor-hid*
Penygwryd	*pen* (head/end).	

pen (head/end). In Snowdonia a valley is named after Cai, one of the knights of King Arthur, the leader of the Welsh, the Cumbrians and the Cornish who defeated the Anglo Saxons and secured fifty years of peace in 6th-century Britain. Gwrhyd Cai is the name of the valley; *gwrhyd* (fathom) is the distance of two arms outstretched. Like most of Arthur's knights, Cai was a superman! Heroes and saints' extraordinary powers are often displayed topographically in Wales by such place names. Penygwryd is at the head of the valley which is the width of Cai's fathom. It's also the name of the hotel used by the climbing team training in Snowdonia for the first successful ascent to the summit of Everest.

grisiau	steps	*grish-eye*
gwaun	moor	*gwine*
llech	slate	*thlake*
llechwedd	slope	*thleck-weth*
llethr	slope	*thleth-air*
maen	stone	*mine*

Penygwryd above Llynnau Mymbyr with Yr Wyddfa (Snowdon) in the background

mawnog	peat-bog	*mow-nogg* ('mow' rhymes with 'now')
moel	bare hilltop	*moil*

Moel Fama (Clwydian Hills) 'Fama' is what everyone says, and that is what is right. But since it isn't a word in contemporary Welsh it's easy to understand the attempts made to turn it into *mamau* (mothers). Even the scholar Sir John Rhys (1883) believed that the meaning was 'the Mother's Mountain', 'the ladies in question being the class of the divine Matres once worshipped by the Celts'.

However, although 'Fama' is fairly closely related to the word *mamau* it's not derived from it. The original derivation of Fama in the Brythonic language was *mamma* 'breast; a round hill like a breast', a description which fits more than one of the hills between Mold and the Vale of Clwyd. The name occurs in Derbyshire as Mam Tor, and in Nottinghamshire as Mamesfeld 1086, which later became Mansfield, and in the city the Romans called Mamucium, which became Mameceaster 923, Mamecestre 1086 and then Manchester.[4]

mynydd	mountain	*munnith*

Mynydd Epynt *epynt* (horse-path). There are several ancient pathways crossing this mountain in Breconshire, and these were favoured by the drovers on their way to London and Kent until the end of the 19th century. Public access was denied after 1943 when the Ministry of Defence occupied the mountain for weapon training (it still does until the present day) – the infamous Epynt Clearances.

A MOD target on Mynydd Epynt

Pencader (Carmarthenshire) In his *Descriptio Kambriae* (1193) Giraldus Cambrensis (Gerald de Barri; *c*.1146–1223) described how Henry II, during the English king's raid through Wales in 1163, questioned an old Welshman on whether he thought the Welsh would continue to resist the power of England. Speaking in Welsh, he gave this reply: 'This nation, O King, may now, as in former times, be harassed, and in a great measure weakened and destroyed by your and other powers, and it will often prevail by its laudable exertions, but it can never be totally subdued through the wrath of man, unless the wrath of God shall concur. Nor do I think that any other nation than this of Wales, or any other language, whatever may hereafter come to pass, shall on the day of severe judgement before the Supreme Judge, answer for this corner of the earth.' The old man's defiant but dignified reply, one of the classic statements of Welsh patriotism, is inscribed on a memorial which was erected in the village under the auspices of Plaid Cymru in 1952.

pen + **cader**	(lit. chair, but used for hill or mountain tops)	
pennau	tops, ends	*penn-eye*
poncyn	hillock	*ponn-kinn*
rhedyn	bracken	*reddinn*
rhiw	slope	*roo*
rhos	moor	*rauss*
rhyl	the hill	*rhil*

Rhyl Y Rhyl is one of the most popular coastal towns in northern Wales. The name is an old one, going back at least 700 years. There is a reference in 1301 to *Ryhull*, to *del Hull* in

Norman archway, Rhosili church

1302, *Hullhouse* in 1351, *Yr hill* in 1578, *Tre-yr-hyll* in 1612 and *Rhyll* in 1660.

What we have here in all probability is the English word *hill* (also meaning hillock) in its Old English form *hyll* or else in one of its Middle English forms. We can compare it with the *hull* of *Solihull* in Birmingham – *hull* here being a form for *hill*.

But wait a moment, some of you may say. The *hull* in Solihull refers to quite a sizeable hillock – i.e. the hill to the south of the church – whereas Y Rhyl in northern Wales is situated in a flat plain, without a hillock near it. True, in the strict geographical sense. But before rejecting the above ('hill', 'hillock') explanation, consider this – that *hyll* or *hull* in English could mean a quite small rise of land in the middle of a plain.

It's possible that that was the original meaning of Y Rhyl in Flintshire. The early English referred to the rise of land towards the mouth of the river Clwyd as a *hull*, and before long *Hull* became the name of the spot. This name was adopted by the Welsh inhabitants of the area, and the Welsh definite article *yr* was added in front of it. *Hull* became *Yr hull* or *Yr hill* and then *rhyl* – that is, a half-'cymricised' English name.

tocyn	small heap	*tockinn*
wyddfa	tomb	*ooith-vah* ('ah' as in 'ah!')

Yr Wyddfa (Snowdon) from Afon Glaslyn

Rivers and Crossings

afon   river   *avvonn*

Afon Dyfrdwy, River Dee   This is one of the oldest river names in Britain. The ancient Celts believed strongly in the divinity of rivers. Aerfen, the goddess of war, was the goddess of the river Dee and there are references in medieval Welsh literature to Llyn Tegid (Bala Lake, the source of the river Dee) as Llyn Aerfen. They also believed that the personal names of the gods were too sacred for everyday use and so referred to Aerfen and to the river with a word which meant 'the goddess, the holy one'. This Celtic word was recorded by Ptolemy as Deova, and in later Welsh as *dwy* (which can be seen in the rivers Dwyfor and Dwyfach, the suffixes *fawr* and *fach* meaning 'large' and 'small'). The Roman fort at Chester was called Deva. This became the form which gave us Dee today. There are several Dees in Scotland too, which all testify to the Celtic divinity of rivers.

In Welsh another word was added in front of the *dwy*, the word which gives us *dwfr* 'water' and *dyfroedd* 'waters' in modern Welsh (and also the name Dover). In fact the modern Welsh name Dyfrdwy is close to the original elements of what is in modern Welsh '*dyfroedd dwyfol*' 'sacred waters'.

Was this memorial to the goddess of war a prophesy of future battles? Certainly the instability of the river Dee as

Afon Llwchwr – an important crossing since Roman times

a boundary between Wales and England caused fierce conflict. As Giraldus Cambrensis noted, there was a belief that the country which lost land because of the erosion of the banks would also lose any battle which followed such conflict.[4]

banc	bank	*bank*
carrog	torrent	*karrogg*
cymer	confluence	*kummair*
dŵr	water	*dooer*
Dyfnant	deep river/hollow	*duvv-nant*
ffos	ditch	*fauss*
ffrwd	stream	*frood*
ffynnon	well	*funnonn*
glan	Usually *glan* and a river name gives the sense of a place 'on the bank of a river' e.g. Glan + Aman = Glanaman; Glan + dyfi = Glandyfi. It also has the meaning of 'edge/brink/shore' and sometimes 'rising ground/hillside'. Glanyferi (Ferryside) – 'at the shore of the ferry'.	
pistyll	waterfall	*pistill* (*ll* – see page 16)
pont	bridge	*pont*

Pontypridd (south-eastern) Rhondda Cynon Taf; industrial town at the confluence of the rivers Taff and Rhondda on the A470.

Here, in 1856, the words of 'Hen Wlad fy Nhadau', which later became the Welsh national anthem, were written by Evan James (Ieuan ap Iago; 1809–78); his son James James (Iago ap Ieuan; 1833–1902) composed the music. The anthem is sung wherever Welsh people gather:

The plaque which commemorates them is on the gable-

Pont yr Afanc, Afon Conwy

end of the last building in Mill Street, but it can be seen only from Sardis Road. The nearby Welsh primary school is known as Ysgol Evan James. A bronze monument to father and son, the work of W. Goscombe John, was erected in Ynys Angharad Park, on the east bank of the Taff near the old bridge, in 1930.

Y Bont-faen; Pen-y-bont (Cowbridge; Bridgend) Bridges have had an enormous effect on the settlements, economy, politics – and place names – of Wales. In saying this I'm not referring to large, impressive structures such as the one over the Severn, or the Menai Bridge; I'm thinking rather of the hundreds of much smaller and older bridges that made it possible for our long-gone ancestors to travel across the country to the market and the fair.

One useful aid in seeking to frame a map of these old bridges is place names containing the word *pont* – for example names like Pen-y-bont ar Ogwr ('end of the bridge on the river Ogwr') and Y Bont-faen ('the bridge of stone').

There was a bridge in the locality of Y Bont-faen well over 700 years ago, somewhere near the place where the old Roman road from Cardiff to Neath crossed the river Ddawan (Thaw). In documents dated 1262–3 there was a reference to the place under the name Covbruge/Coubrigge, the Old English forms of Cowbridge, or bridge for cows.

What sort of bridge was it, I wonder, and why was it called Cowbridge? I don't know the answer. But around it, in the 14th century, grew up one of the largest towns in Wales. Later on, another bridge was built – a stone one; and

Rhaeadr Ddu, Maentwrog

this gave us the Welsh name, Y Bont-faen ('the bridge of stone'), which occurs around 1500.

Pen-y-bont ar Ogwr is a considerably 'younger' place than Y Bont-faen. In the Middle Ages there is no mention of it. There were two settlements or villages – Newcastle towards the west and Nolton or Oldcastle towards the east, with the river Ogwr between them.

Somewhere around 1435 or a little afterwards a four-arched bridge was constructed. Soon a few houses went up at its eastern end, and these came to be called Bridgend, or in Welsh, Pen-y-bont. It was a very small place until the post-1820 industrialisation. After that Pen-y-bont grew swiftly, swallowing up Newcastle and Nolton.

pwll	pit, pool	*pooll* (*ll* – see page 16)
rhaeadr	waterfall	*rye-addar*

Rhaeadr Gwy (Rhayader) (central) There used to be a waterfall on the Gwy (Wye) river but there are only rapids here now, a result – it's said – of the cutting of a water channel in the river during the erection of a bridge in 1780.

rhyd	ford	*reed*

Rhyd-y-mwyn

Rhyd-y-mwyn means 'the ford of the ore'. The village is squeezed tightly between the river Alun and the main road from Mold to Denbigh. That road doesn't cross the river, let alone go through a ford, indeed it avoids the village.

But there is another road in Rhyd-y-mwyn, the lane from the main road towards Pant-y-mwyn, which does cross the river Alun. Here then was the ford ('*a foard on Alyn*' as Lhuyd put it *c.*1700). The minerals (lead in particular) were found in Pant-y-mwyn and other places nearby. It's quite possible that large quantities of ore were carried along this lane, through the ford in Rhyd-y-mwyn and on towards Halkyn or Northop and the river Dee. At one time, incidentally, the place appears to have been called Rhydeurgain, echoing the Welsh name for Northop, Llaneurgain.[4]

sarn	causeway	*sarn*
sgwd	waterfall	*sgood*
ynys	island	*unniss*

Ynys-lwyd (south-eastern) *Ynys* can mean a meadow in a meandering river or dry, rising ground in the middle of a marsh, as well as the more usual meaning of 'island'. The second element *llwyd* above is also not as straight forward as it appears. It could be *llwyd* (russet/brown), suggesting the colour of the meadow (*llwyd* can vary in shades from gray, faint, pale to russet or brown; it can also refer to poor land). On the other hand, it can mean 'holy' as in 'Maen Llwyd' (holy stone) and yet again it could be a personal name, maybe the surname of the original owner, Llwyd.

ystum	bend in river	*uss-timm*
ystwyth	winding	*uss-tooith*

Valleys

cwm   mountain, valley   *koomm*

Cwmbach (south-eastern Wales) *Bach* is an adjective meaning 'little' or 'small'. Cwm-bach was the name given to a farmstead 'in the little valley'. With the development of the Aberdare Canal (1812–1900), coal pits were opened in the area and the former rural valley became an industrial settlement, taking its name from the original farm. In 1860, the first Co-operative in Wales was formed at Bridge Road, Cwm-bach.

cymau   mountain valleys   *kumm-eye*

Cymau

The word *cwm* (plural *cymoedd* or *cymau*) means 'valley' and between Caergwrle and Ffrith there are a number of valleys (some very steep) leading down from the southern slopes of Hope Mountain towards the banks of the river Cegidog. The name describes the area in general rather than the village. It's referred to as 'y Cymau' to this day (which explains the forms *Accymey* and *Accumey*) just as we refer to 'the Valleys' in south Wales.

The plural *cymau*, although rarer than *cymoedd*, is common enough. Locally the plural *cyme* also developed, a feature of the local dialect which substitutes *–e* for *–au*. There is another, supposedly Anglicized, variant in *–i* heard in the common local pronunciation, similar to 'Cymmi' and also well evidenced in older documents.[4]

dôl   meadow   *dole*

Dolforwyn castle above the Severn valley

Dolforwyn (central)	*Dôl* and probably a personal name Morein, 'Morein's meadow' (the Welsh *morwyn* [maiden] is unlikely here). It's the site of a castle built by Llywelyn ap Gruffudd, Prince of Wales, in 1277 to defend southern Gwynedd against Norman invasions along the upper Severn valley. Llywelyn's dream was that Dolforwyn would become his national seat, growing to be a central capital for the whole of Wales.	
dolau	meadows	*doll-eye*
dyffryn	valley	*duff-rinn*
Dyffryn (south-eastern)	In Cwm Cynon, the name Dyffryn has pastoral connections – it was the name of a farm, mill and woodland on the valley floor. It also has industrial links – here was the vast Powell Duffryn coalmine.	
glyn	valley	*glinn*
Glyn-y-groes (north-eastern)	*Vale Crucis* abbey near Llangollen. The glen was once dominated by a high cross on the Eliseg Pillar erected in the 9th century to commemorate Welsh victories over the Mercian armies. The cross (*y groes*) was once some twenty feet high, but in the 17th century Cromwell troops pulled it down and smashed its noble cross. It was re-erected, shorter and without its cross, in 1779. It stands on a Bronze Age burial mound and gave its name to the glen and later to a medieval Cistercian abbey founded by the prince of Powys in 1200.	
llawr	ground	*thlowr* (rhymes with 'hour')
llyn	lake	*thlinn*
melin	mill	*mellinn*
nant	brook	*nant*

Glyn-y-groes abbey, near Llangollen

Nantlle

Nantlle, in Gwynedd, in that form, is the name seen on signposts, and the spoken form is Nantlle or Nanlle. But its full form is Nant Lleu: that is, 'Lleu's Valley', which immediately suggests all sorts of connections.

Lleu is the name of the central character in the Fourth Branch of the Mabinogi, and after being betrayed by his wife Blodeuwedd, he turns into an eagle and flies away. The magician Gwydion finds him in the oak wood of Dyffryn Nantlle and turns him back into a man.

The name Lleu is interesting. At root it's identical with the *lleu* which is the first part of *lleuad* ('moon') and the second part of *golau*, 'light'. Trace the word behind it to Brythonic – the Celtic language from which Welsh sprang – and still further to the Celtic dialects which were spoken across extensive parts of Europe before the Romans, and you come to the form *lug* – a word cognate with *lux*, which means 'light' in Latin.

Lugus, god of light, was one of the leading divinities of the ancient Celts. When they named a fort or important town, they often did so in his honour, calling it 'dinas Lleu' – or rather, according to the usage of their language at the time, *Lugudunum*. There was more than one town of this name on the Continent, and as the language of each area changed in the course of hundreds and hundreds of years so the name changed also. In the south of France it became Lyon, in northern France Laon, and in Holland, Leyden. Every one of these towns was originally a stronghold dedicated to the Celtic god Lugus, or Lleu.

Returning to *Lugudunum* for a moment, I said that *lug*

has become *lleu* in Welsh and that *dun* has become *din*, as in *dinas* ('city'). Given the existence of a *Lugudunum* in Wales, you would expect it to have developed into *Lleudin*. Take this name and reverse the order of its elements and there you have *Dinlleu*. It's the ancient fort Dinas Dinlle in the vicinity of Caernarfon, not far from Nantlle.

Place names often speak volumes, and names like Nantlle and Dinas Dinlle certainly do that. They whisper to us of the ancient Celtic god Lleu, whose powers were venerated by our ancestors 2,500 years ago.[5]

pant	valley/dip	*pant*
ystrad	vale	*uss-tradd*

Ystrad Fflur Latin – *Strata Florida* (central)

The ruined abbey near Pontrhydfendigaid, Ceredigion, was once one of the most celebrated in Wales; it was the burial-place of the Princes of the House of Dinefwr. There is a splendid memorial inside the walls, inscribed in Welsh and Latin and erected by the Honourable Society of Cymmrodorion in 1951, to the memory of the great poet Dafydd ap Gwilym (*fl.*1315/20–1350/70). He is traditionally said to be buried under a yew tree at the front of the church; the spot is marked by a very shabby stone with painted lettering and is easily missed. It should be noted – without, of course, taking sides in the argument – that the abbey at Talley near Llandeilo also has a claim to being the poet's last resting-place.

Trees and Shrubs

bedwen	birch	*bedd-wenn*
celli (gelli)	grove	*kethly*
Y Gelli (Hay-on-Wye)		
celynnen	holly tree	*kell-unnenn*

Pantycelyn (south western) A farmhouse, *pant* and *y celyn* ('the holly') which is also the fond nickname given to the prolific hymn-writer William Williams (1717–91), who lived there after his marriage *c.*1748. He was one of the leaders of the Methodist movement in Wales, and its major poet, some of which have been translated. The English hymn for which Williams Pantycelyn is most famous is the one usually sung – more often at rugby matches than in chapel these days – to the tune 'Cwm Rhondda':

> Guide me, O Thou great Jehovah,
> Pilgrim through this barren land;
> I am weak, but Thou art mighty,
> Hold me with thy powerful hand.
> Bread of Heaven, bread of Heaven,
> Feed me till I want no more!

Celynnog, nr Llanrhaeadr-ym-Mochnant The ending '*og*' usually means 'having abundance of'. In this case, *celyn* + *og* means 'a place which has an abundance of holly'.

'Drain' – thorns, Clwydian hills

Clynnog Fawr (north-western) A condensed version of 'Celynnog'. The ornate church at Clynnog Fawr, dedicated to St Beuno in the 7th century, was once an important place on the pilgrims' road to Bardsey. There is also 'Clynnog Fechan' ('little Clynnog') in Anglesey.

clawdd	dyke, ditch	*klowthe* (rhymes with 'mouthe')
coed	trees, wood	*koid*

Bolgoed, nr Loughor, Glamorgan In Welsh *bol/bola* means 'belly'. Bolgoed would mean either 'wood in a cavity/hollow' or, more likely in this case, 'wood on a prominent mound'.

coety	house in wood	*koity*
cog	cuckoo	*kaug*
collen	hazel tree	*koth-lenn*
cyll	hazel trees	*kith*
derw	oaks	*derroo*
derwen	oak	*dair-wenn*
drain	thorns	*drine*
ffawydd	beech	*fow-ith*

Ffawyddog (The Foothog) Compare with 'Celynnog'. This is a place which has an abundance of beech trees.

grug	hillock, heather	*greeg*
gwern	swamp	*gwairn*
helyg	willows	*helligg*
llannerch	glade	*thlann-airk*
llwyn	grove, bush	*thlooinn*

Llwyn-onn (south-eastern) The village takes its name from the original farm/homestead called after an ash bush/shrub/copse or grove. *Onn* is the plural of *onnen* – ash tree.

Heather (grug) on Preseli, Pembrokeshire

mawnog	peat bog	*mow-nogg* ('mow' rhymes with 'now')
on, onn	ash trees	*onn*
onnen	ash tree	*onnenn*
Maesyronnen (central)	*Maes* indicates an open field – therefore, the field of the ash tree. The best-known farm which carries this name was also the site of an old Baptist chapel established in 1696.	
perllan	orchard	*pairth-lann*
perth	hedge, bush	*pairth*
Perth-hir (south-eastern)	'long wood, long bush'	
pren	timber	*prenn*
rhedyn	bracken	*reddinn*
wig	wood	*weeg*
Penwig (central)	This is the name of one of the beaches at Ceinewydd (Newquay), Ceredigion, (the nearest to the harbour). It lies under a slope of thorn trees – 'at the head of the grove'.	
ysgawen	elder tree	*uss-kowenn* ('kow' rhymes with 'cow')
ywen	yew	*ow-enn*
yw	yews	*eeow* (rhymes with 'new')

Maesyronnen, an early nonconformist chapel in Powys

aber
Aberafan (Aberavon)

river mouth   *abbair*

Aber is the Welsh word for a place where a river flows into the sea, or where a smaller river joins a larger one. It's a very common element at the beginning of place names in Wales. It's also found in parts of Scotland – for example, in Aberdeen at the mouth of the river Don, and in Arbroath. Aberbrothog was the old form of the latter – namely the place where Bannock Burn flows into the sea.

Aberafan is the place where the river Afan has its outlet to the sea. The forms *Afan* and *Afen* occur early on for the river name, but no one rightly knows how to explain them.

Some have supposed that *Afan* was a form of the word *afon*, 'river'. The naming *Ecclesia Abbona*, i.e. 'church on the river', occurs as early as 1348, and the English antiquary John Leland mentions *Aber-Avon* in 1536–9. But although the form Aberavon is very old, it's a false form. The correct name is Aberafan.

Port Talbot (i.e. the docks at Aberafan Harbour) is a late name. It was coined around 1836, when the docks were newly built to export coal and iron from the estuary of the river Afan. The docks took their name from the Talbots, an English family who had inherited the old estates of Margam and Pen-rhys through marriage. Port Talbot was just one of the English names containing *port* which were coined

Abermaw, where the Mawddach flows to the sea

during the 19th century, when new ports were being built along the coasts of Wales.

Others include Port Penrhyn in Bangor, the harbour which was constructed for the export of slate from Penrhyn Quarry. Then there is Port Dinorwig in Y Felinheli (literally 'salt-water mill' or 'tidal mill', but renowned for exporting slate from Dinorwig Quarry). And there's also Porthmadog which was named after the local tradition of Ynys Madog – an island from where the 12th-century adventurer Madog ab Owain Gwynedd sailed to discover America – and which is also connected to William Alexander Madocks, the man who caused an embankment or cob to be raised across Traeth Mawr ('great strand') and then later built a harbour there.

Another foreign name of the same type is Portmeirion, the name of the pseudo-Italian village which Clough Williams-Ellis created in the vicinity of Traeth Bach ('little strand') near Penrhyndeudraeth, the peninsula between Traeth Bach and Traeth Mawr – i.e. 'peninsula of the two (*dau*) strands'.[5]

(and for an inland use of 'aber'):

Aberaman   *Aber* = the mouth of a river or stream, where it opens out into the sea, or where it runs into another river.

Aman   A Celtic river name, from *Amanw*, related to the Welsh word *banw* – a pig or pigling, and refers to a river rooting through the ground.

Bannow in Wexford (Ireland), along with Ammanford, Glanaman, and Brynaman, Carmarthenshire, contain the same animal element.

cf. the rivers Twrch ('boar'), Gwys ('pig', 'sow') and Hwch ('sow') – appropriate names for wild rivers that burrow their way through earth and stones.

The name Aberaman refers to the place where the river Aman flows into the river Cynon.[3]

awel	breeze	*ow-ell* ('ow' as in 'now')
awelon	breezes	*ow-ellonn* ('ow' as in 'now')
bae	bay	*bye*
Bae Colwyn		

Bae Colwyn is the second largest town in northern Wales, after Wrecsam (Wrexham).

It's not hard to explain the *Bae* part of the name. The Welsh version of the English *bay*, it was tacked on to *Colwyn* in order to tell visitors from England that the place boasted a fine beach. The addition dates from the 1860s and 1870s, when our northern coastline was beginning to sprout holiday centres.

What about Colwyn itself? There was a word *colwyn* in Welsh whose original meaning was 'young animal'. It was used of a young dog, especially a male one. 'Pretty little doggies to amuse the women' was the pleasing definition of *colwyn* by Thomas Wiliems of Trefriw (1545/6–1622) in his dictionary. The word also appears in an old saying, 'Happy is the little dog on his master's knee'. But what has all this to do with the name of a town in the north?

Well, in Welsh you often find rivers named after animals. There's a river Twrch ('boar'), for example, in both Ystalyfera and Llanuwchllyn; a river Hwch ('sow') near Llanberis; while *banw*, a word for a young pig, lies behind the names of the river Banw (in Montgomeryshire), and,

ultimately, of the Aman (Carmarthenshire) and the Ogwen (Bethesda, Arfon).

Colwyn also came to denote streams or rivulets. There are several of them – one rising on the slopes of Yr Wyddfa (Snowdon) and flowing down to Beddgelert, one flowing into the river Cerist near Caersws, and another into the river Efyrnwy in Dyffryn Meifod.

There is also a river Colwyn in the district of Llaneilian-yn-Rhos (another name for it being the river Penmaen). This river name became that of a township and then, in due course, that of the towns, Old Colwyn and Bae Colwyn.[5]

cei	quay	*kay*
clogwyn	cliff	*klog-winn*
môr-forwyn	mermaid	*mor-vor-winn*
gwynt	wind	*gwint*
haul	sun	*hile*
heli	salt water	*helly*
maen	stone	*mine*
min	edge	*minn*
môr	sea	*mor*
morfa	marsh	*mor-vah* ('ah' as in 'ah!')
ogof	cave	*oggovv*
penarth	headland	*penn-arth*
penrhyn	headland	*penn-rinn*
porth	harbour/cove	*porth*

Porth-cawl Who would imagine that the *cawl* in the name Porth-cawl in Glamorgan is the same as the *cawl* (broth) that we eat for dinner? Yet that's the fact of the matter. The word *cawl* was borrowed into Welsh from the Latin *caulis*, a word for a cabbage stalk. It was ultimately the same Latin word that gave the English the *cauli* in 'cauliflower', the *cole* in 'coleslaw', and also the word 'kale'.

It's a combination of *porth* ('port', 'ferry-point') and *cawl*.

In Welsh, *cawl* can mean 'cabbage', (*bresych, cabaetsen*). It also occurs in a word for a kind of broth containing this plant.

There is another plant which the English call 'sea-kale' and which grows near seashores. In his *Welsh Botanology* of 1813, Hugh Davies says that it's to be found on the shore in Penmon and Llanddona (Anglesey), but adds that it's a fairly rare plant.

There must be a lot of sea kale growing on the shore in Drenewydd yn Notais (Newton Nottage), Glamorgan. *Cawl* or *cawl môr* used to be the name for it. The harbour or seashore where this was plentiful came to be called *Porthcawl* – exactly as the shore at Llanfwrog in Anglesey came to be called *Porthdelysg* – because a kind of edible seaweed, *delysg*, was to be found there. Incidentally, it's thought that the stalk of sea-kale is tasty to eat.[5]

ton	wave	*tonn*
traeth	beach	*trye-th*
trwyn	promontory	*trooinn*
ynys	island	*unniss*

The cliffs of Penrhyn Govan, Pembrokeshire

Farms and Homesteads

beudy	cowshed	*baidy*
bod	dwelling	*bawd*
brain	crows	*brine*
brân	crow	*brahn* ('ah' as in 'ah!')
buarth	yard	*bee-arth*
bwthyn	cottage	*boothinn*
caban	hut	*kabbann*
cae	field	*kye*
Cae-Garw (south-eastern)	*cae* = a field; *garw* = coarse, rough, rugged, harsh[3]	
cartre	home	*kar-tray*
cartref	home	*kar-trevv*
cegin	kitchen	*kegginn*
cennin	leeks	*kenninn*
clwyd	hurdle/gate	*klooidd*
diserth	wilderness	*dissairth*
efail	smithy	*evvile* (rhymes with 'smile')
erw	acre	*erroo*
ffin	boundary	*finn*
gwalch	hawk	*gwalc* (rhymes with 'talc')
Hafod	Welsh *haf*, summer + *bod*, residence, abode.	
		ha vode ('o' as in 'door')[3]

hafod = 'summer dwelling; upland farm, occupied in the summer only; dairy house'. cf. *hafdre* and *hafoty*.
hendre, *hendy* were the Welsh names for the main or winter farmhouses.

hafod, *hafdre* (as in *Ynys hafdre* > Ynysawdre, Tondu) and *hafoty* were related to the farmhouses that were used in summer only, when the cattle and sheep were able to graze on the highland pasture.

Hafodyrynys (south-eastern) 'Summer-dwelling at the water-meadow', with *hafod* typically an upland farm occupied in summer when stock was moved onto higher pastures. In Welsh, *ynys* usually means 'island' but in many parts of southern Wales it was used for 'a raised area in water-meadows' and, by extension, 'water-meadow'. A former grange of Llantarnam Abbey.[13]

hafoty	summer house	*havvotty*
hendref (**hendre**)	winter home	*henn-drevv*
iarth	yard	*yarth*
llaeth	milk	*thlye-th*
lle	place	*thlay*
lluest	cabin	*thlee-est*
maes	field	*mice*

Maesgwenith 'Wheat field': In Welsh, *maes* + *gwenith* ('wheat').[14]

march	horse	*mark*
meirch	horses	*mairk*
moch	pigs	*mauk*
mur	wall	*meer*
nos	night	*nauss*
parc	field	*park*
pentref (**pentre**)	village	*penn-trevv*

Pentre'r-felin (common throughout the country)

'The mill village': *pentre(f)*, def. art. *y* attached to the *–e* as *'r* and *melin*, 'mill'. *Melin* is feminine and mutates after the def. art. to produce *felin*.

porfa	pasture	*por-vah* ('ah'; as in 'ah!')
pridd	soil	*preethe*
rhandir	allotment	*rann-deer*
sticill	stile	*stickill* (*ll* – see page 16)
tir	land	*teer*
tref (**tre**)	town	*trave*

Tre Beirdd (north-eastern) This means 'the poets' farm'. In the Middle Ages in Wales, poets were patronised by the great families and according to the Laws of Hywel Dda, such a family poet had the right to hold land without paying rent. Often such lands still bear the names of the poets. In Anglesey, for example, there was Tre Walchmai (the village of Gwalchmai today); Gwalchmai was the chief poet at the 12th-century court of Prince Gruffydd ap Cynan. Also in Anglesey you find Llanfihangel Tre'r Beirdd. It's a pity that we know nothing more about these poets of Mold.[4]

twlc	pigsty	*toolk*
tŷ	house	*tee*
tyddyn	small farm	*tuthinn* ('uth' as 'oth' in 'other')
ty'n	small farm	*teen*
ysgubor	barn	*uss-kibbor*

Ysgubor-wen (south-eastern) also general.

Welsh *ysgubor* + *gwen* (mutated to *wen*).
ysgubor = barn; building in which grain, hay etc. is stored.
Dialect forms are *sgibor*, *sgipor*, plural *ysguboriau*, *sgibora*.
Cornish 'sciber', prof. > Engl. 'skipper' (barn, outbuilding).
gwen = white. Feminine form of *gwyn*.

Hafod Wen – hill farm in Meirionnydd

Llan

llan	church	*thlann*

Llanwynno (south-eastern) Welsh *llan* + Gwynno

Llan = (parish) church

Gwynno = personal name (saint)

Gwynno's church

There are over six hundred and thirty *llan* place names in Wales, yet *Llanwynno* is the only example of a *llan* place name in the Cynon valley. The word *llan* has an interesting history.

As both English and Welsh originated from the Indo-European languages that spread from the north of India and across Europe, there is a close relationship between the Welsh word *llan* and the English *land*. The original meaning of the word was 'a piece of land'. It's a very old word, dating back to Brythonic – the ancient tongue from which Welsh sprang – and before that to Celtic, the mother of Brythonic. Ultimately it comes from the same source as the name *Landes* in southern France and the word *land* in English.

In Welsh, *llan* came to mean a piece of land enclosed for the purpose of keeping something safe. It's present in *perllan*, a piece of land enclosed for cultivating apple trees, and in *gwinllan*, a piece of land for cultivating vines.

Llan also became the Welsh word for a piece of land enclosed and consecrated by one of the early Christian

The old church at Llangelynnin, near Conwy

saints for the purpose of building a church, and subsequently it came to signify 'church' on its own. That, for the most part, is its meaning in place names. Very soon however, the word was used for 'an enclosed cemetery', then for the church inside the cemetery and finally for the land served by that church and its vicar, (ie.) – the parish.

Very often *llan* is followed by the name of an early saint or the patron saint of the parish, with the initial consonant of the saint's name mutated because it's the second element of a compound word – St Teilo in Llan*deilo*, Tudno in Llan*dudno* and so on. Don't inquire too much about the history of these early saints: we know very little of it as regards most of them.

Gwynno is the patron saint of Llanwynno and is said to be one of the three patron saints of Llantrisant (along with Illtyd and Tyfodwg) as well as being one of the five saints of Llanpumsaint (Gwyn, Gwynno, Gwynoro, Celynin and Ceitho). His name is also seen in Maenor Gwynno (the parish of Vaynor) near Merthyr Tudful.[3]

Llanrwst The old form of the name was Llanrwrst – *llan*, 'consecrated land', 'church', plus the saint's name *Gwrwst* – which, in Welsh, corresponds to *Fergus* in Irish. But we know virtually nothing about Gwrwst himself.[5]

Llanfair Pwllgwyngyll (northern) A village on the A5, about 3m west of Menai Bridge. The full name of the village is a spoof meant to entertain visitors:

Llanfairpwllgwyngyllgogerychwyrndrobwyllllantysiliogogog och (trans. The church of St Mary in a hollow of white hazel near the rapid whirlpool and the church of St Tysilio near a red cave). The name, said to be the longest place name in the countries of Britain, is thought to have been concocted by a tailor from Menai Bridge in the mid 19th century.

Llanuwchllyn (northern) *llan* + *uwch* (above) *llyn* (lake)

Renowned as one of the most cultured villages in rural Wales and the birthplace of prose writer and scholar Owen Morgan Edwards (1858–1920). He was educated at the village school now named after him, where he experienced the use of the Welsh Not, a device meant to prevent pupils from speaking their native language. He continued his education at the Calvinistic Methodist College in Bala, the University College of Wales, Aberystwyth, and Lincoln College, Oxford. He returned to Wales in 1907 on his appointment as Chief Inspector of Schools and made his home first at Tremaran and then at Neuadd Wen (the Welsh for white hall), a large house in the village, where he died. His extensive literary output was written in Welsh for the benefit of the ordinary people of Wales, whom he tended to idealize. Besides his many books, he founded the influential periodical *Cymru* and *Cymru'r Plant*, a magazine for the children of Wales.

Churches and Saints

abaty   abbey   *ab-attee*

Abbeycwmhir: Abaty Cwm-hir (central) A modern name, coined in the 18th century, probably about the time that Sir William Fowler erected St Mary's church (rebuilt in 1866) near his mansion Abbeycwmhir Hall and the ruins of the abbey of Cwm-hir established by the Cistercians in 1143. The valley (*cwm*) is narrow and twisting rather than 'long'. Lewis Morris 1796 called the abbey Mynachlog y Cwm Hir (*mynachlog*: 'monastery') but most Welsh sources call it simply Y Cwm Hir, 'the long valley'.[12]

Here, on 11 December 1282, the decapitated body of Llywelyn ap Gruffudd, the last prince of independent Wales, was secretly buried by monks of the Cistercian Order; his head was sent to London to be exhibited at Cheapside as a sign of Edward I's conquest of Wales. The Prince's death was lamented in a powerful elegy by Gruffudd ab yr Ynad Coch (*fl.* 1277–82) expressing the utter dismay felt by the Welsh at the end of the royal house of Gwynedd (trans.):

Why, O my God, does the sea not cover the land?
Why are we left to linger?

The abbey, once the largest in Wales, was demolished at the Dissolution of 1542. A marble slab marking the spot where the Prince is said to lie buried is the focus for an annual gathering of Welsh patriots.

bedd   grave   *bathe*
beddau   graves   *beth-eye*

bendigaid	blessed	*benn-diggide* (rhymes with 'side')
betws **Betws**	oratory	*bettooss*

There are two identical words *betws* in Welsh – but their meanings are very different.

One is an old homegrown term for a fairly steep slope or hillside where there is a thick growth of small hazel, thorn and birch trees – in fact the Welsh name *bedw*, for the birch tree, lies at the root of this term. Add the old plural ending *-os* to *bedw* and that gives you *bedwos*, a version of this being the name of a place – Bedwas – close to Caerffili (Caerphilly). You could translate that into English as 'birch grove'.

In speech *bedwos* became *betwos* in some districts, the *d* hardening to *t* in front of *w*, exactly as in *pysgotwr* (for *pysgodwr*), 'fisherman'. Later on the *o* in *betwos* was lost, to give *betws* as a term in parts of north-eastern and eastern Wales for a wooded slope. 'Mae y tir yn un betws', they said there in the old days – that is, 'the ground is all over-run with underwood and small trees'.

Of purely English origin is the other word *betws*, the one that means 'church' as in the saying 'y byd a'r betws' ('the world and the church'). That comes from an old form for 'bead house' in English – the place where you went to pray. But 'necklace' is the meaning of 'beads' in English, some of you might say. Yes, certainly – nowadays. To begin with, however, the meaning of 'bead' was 'to pray'. The sense of 'necklace' came about because in the act of praying people used to count tiny balls on a string.

So a 'bead house' was a house into which one turned in

order to say prayers, a small chapel or oratory as an adjunct to the parish church. The word itself was borrowed into Welsh as *betws* – the old form 'house' giving – *ws* or – *hws* (as with *becws*, 'bakehouse', and *warws*, 'warehouse'), and the *h* in *hws* hardening the *d* to *t*. Various old 'chapels of ease' bear the name *Betws* in Wales – Betws Gwerful Goch outside Corwen being one example.

One interesting thing about this name is that from it we learn that one *Gwerful* gave her name to the church.

Some of the genealogies make mention of Gwerful, daughter of Cynan ab Owain Gwynedd, adding that she was buried at Dinmael. King Owain Gwynedd died in 1170, and his son Cynan in 1174. That means that Gwerful flourished towards the year 1200 or a little before that. It appears that she encouraged the building of a chapel or small church and gave Betws Gwerful Goch its name.

capel	chapel	*kappell*
cist	coffer	*kist*
clafdy	hospital	*klavv-dy*
clas	monastic community	*claas*
Clas Garmon		

In Welsh, *clas* meant 'monastic community, convent' and occurs quite commonly in Wales. This example refers to the *clas* at Saint Harmon but *Clas Garmon* is likely to mean not '*clas* of St Garmon' but '*clas* in Saint Harmon (parish)'.[12]

croes	cross (road)	*kroiss*
Dewi	David	*day-wy*
eglwys	church	*egg-lewis*
Mair	Mary	*mire*

Betws-y-coed

merthyr	martyr	*mair-theer*
Mihangel	Michael	*mee-hang-ell*
mynach	monk	*munnak*

Tirmynech (central) — 'The monks' land': *tir*, def. art. *y* and *meneich*, later *myneich*, plural of *mynach*, 'monk'. This was an area, later regarded as a manor, carved out of Ystradmarchell, centred on and held by the Cistercian monastery of *Strata Marcella*.[11]

mynachlog	monastery	*munn-ak-log*

Mynachlog-ddu (south-western) *mynachlog* + *du* (black). A small village in the Preseli hills in Pembrokeshire. The poet Waldo Williams (1904–71) lived here as a boy when his father was headmaster of the village school. The fact that Welsh was the first language of the inhabitants proved a decisive influence on his later writing. Most of his poetry, collected in the volume *Dail Pren* (1956), was written during the 1940s and was inspired by the district. He is one of the greatest Welsh poets of the 20th century. Pacifist and mystic, he wrote on universal themes such as the brotherhood of all men and women, but his work is rooted in the Preseli hills and in a vision of a free, Welsh-speaking, unbelligerent and Christian Wales. In his poem '*Pa beth yw Dyn?*' he asks and answers a number of fundamental questions about society and the individual, such as (trans.):

> What is being a nation? A talent
> Springing from the heart.
> And love of country? Keeping house
> Among a cloud of witnesses.

A standing stone near Mynachlog-ddu

A commemorative stone was erected near the village in 1978. Waldo taught at a number of primary schools in Pembrokeshire between 1928 and 1942, including those at Dinas, Solva, Camrose, Dale, Cresselly, Carew, Redberth, Rudbaxton and Cas-mael. The poet is buried at Blaenconin, where his tombstone bears the words, '*Gwyn eu byd y tangnefeddwyr*' (Blessed are the peacemakers).

Pedr	Peter	*peddair*
plwyf	parish	*plooivv*
saint	saints	*sign-t*
sant	saint	*sant*
trindod	trinity	*trinn-dodd*
twr	tower	*tooer*
ysbyty	hospital	*uss-putty*

Ysbyty, Mynydd Tre-ysbyty (central) Welsh *ysbyty*, 'hospital, hospice', 'a hospice for pilgrims' according to Ellis, established by the Knights Hospitallers perhaps *c*.1200. The hill Mynydd St John is *Ffridd St John* 1838 with *Cefn-tre-Yspytty* extending from its west side. *Tre-* is simply Welsh *tre(f)* in the sense of township; *Ysbyty* was a township of Llanwddyn parish.[11]

The church of Dewi, St David – the patron saint of Wales

Castles and Forts

beili	yard	*bailey*
brenin	king	*brenninn*
caer	fort	*kyre*

Caerfyrddin (Carmarthen) The earliest written evidence we possess for place names in Wales consists of forms recorded by some of the Greek and Roman authors of the ancient world.

There is the mathematician and astronomer of Alexandria, Claudius Ptolemaeus or Ptolemy. Somewhere around AD 150 he wrote a treatise in Greek, the *Geography*. In it are references to places in Britain – to *Maridunum*, for example.

Maridunum, with *a* in the first syllable, is in Ptolemy's treatise. But scholars who specialise in these matters agree that the *a* is an error for *o*, and that *Moridunum* is the correct name.

Moridunum: that was the name in Brythonic, i.e. the kind of Celtic language that was spoken in Britain 2000 years ago, and the language from which Welsh sprang *via* natural processes.

Let's dwell for a moment on the form *Moridunum*. We can divide it into two words – *mori* and *dunum*. Take the second one, *dunum*. We can forget the ending *–um*. That leaves the stem *dun*, a word meaning 'fort'. In Welsh this changed to *din* – the same *din* as in *dinas* ('city'). Then *mori*. Forget the ending *–i*, which leaves *mor* – an early form of our *môr*, 'sea'.

Moridunum was a combination of words meaning 'sea' and 'fort' respectively. Its meaning was 'fort by the sea', or 'sea fort'.

As Brythonic changed slowly into Welsh, *Moridunum* became *Myrddin*. And at one period in the history of the Welsh language *Myrddin* was the name of the place which was known as *Moridunum* in the time of Ptolemy.

Later on, the fact that the name *Myrddin* already contained within it the word *din* meaning 'fort' was overlooked. So the word *caer* was added to it – unnecessarily – and that brought the name Caerfyrddin into existence.

Other names, like Caergybi (Holyhead) and Caer-gai were a combination of *caer* and a personal name – here Cybi and Cai. It came to be thought that Caerfyrddin was similar – a combination of *caer* with the personal name *Myrddin*. And traditions about the ancient bard and magician of the name Myrddin were linked – quite groundlessly – with the town. But Myrddin's – or Merlin's – is another story, one which it would take a whole book to trace.[5]

Caernarfon

In the tale about Branwen in the Mabinogi, Branwen sends a starling from Ireland to Wales to tell Brân the Blessed, her elder brother, how the Irish are mistreating and punishing her. The starling safely crosses the sea and finds its way to Brân in the midst of his counsellors – and all this, in the words of the tale, in 'Caer Seint in Arfon'.

This was the name of Caernarfon at the time when the tale of Branwen was written – which, of course, was before the building of the great Norman castle we're familiar with on the quay.

The old fort, pre-dating Edward's castle, was the Roman one on the hill near Llanbeblig church – *Segontium* to you and me today, but *Caer Saint* (or *Caer Seint*) to our ancestors.

Yes, to the Romans it was *Segontium*. When they first came to Eryri (Snowdonia), they adopted the name of the river in the Brythonic tongue as that of the fort built by them. That name was *Segonti*, containing the root *seg* and meaning – perhaps – 'flowing strongly'. It's the same root *seg* which is at the beginning of Siguenza, the name of a Spanish town between Madrid and Zarogoza.

In the course of time, as Brythonic changed into Welsh, so *Segonti* changed into *Seint* (or *Saint*). The Welsh called the Roman fort *Caer Seint yn Arfon* and the mouth of the river, where Edward's castle was built, *Aber-seint* – or possibly Aber-sein in everyday speech.

Caer Seint yn Arfon was a mouthful of a name; the next natural step was its contraction. It became *Caer yn Arfon* and, in the spoken language, the single word Caernarfon – which, by now, has been verbally shortened again to C'narfon.

For historians of the language there is one problem in connection with this explanation. Usually an *s* at the beginning of a Brythonic word gives *h* in Welsh. The river called Sabrina in Brythonic gave the name Severn in English, with the *s* remaining. In Welsh, in accordance with the regular characteristics of the language, the name changed to Hafren.

Conwy castle on the river estuary

From *Segonti*, according to this usual pattern, one might have expected *Haint* to be the name of the river. But *Saint* it is. Why the difference? One possible answer is that a form like *Segonti* was part of the everyday speech of Latin-speaking people in Caernarfon long enough for the initial *s* to be retained.

Thus far I have referred without exception to the river *Saint*, and not to the *Seiont*. The fact is that *Seiont* is a 'learned' artificial form based on *Segontium*.[5]

Caerdydd (Cardiff)

Caerdydd is the (Welsh) name of the capital of Wales.

It would be very easy to think that Caerdydd is the combination of *caer*, 'fort', and the Welsh word *dydd* ('day'). This would be a great mistake, and an example of seeking to explain a place name on the basis of its form as it is today, without looking to see what the old form was.

It's true that Caerdydd has been the name for a span of 200 years. But before that it was *Caerdyf*. An old Welsh poet speaks of going

'To Caerdyf and the tavern'.

Our task, then, is to explain the form *Caerdyf*.

Let us take the name Caergybi, the Welsh name for Holyhead. Caergybi was formed from *caer* and the name of the saint *Cybi* – the *c* in Cybi being mutated as a *g* at the beginning of the second element of a compound word, according to the custom in Welsh. In *Caerdyf*, *caer* must have been followed by an original form *Tyf*. But what is *Tyf*?

Talacharn (Laugharne) castle

The river that flows through the capital is called the *Taf*. An old form of this was *Tyf*. The meaning of *Caerdyf*, then, was *caer yr afon Taf* – 'fort of the river Taf'.

In spoken Welsh *Caerdyf* changed to *Caerdydd* – the *f* (or *v*) changing to *dd*. In English, *Caerdyf* was preserved, but with the Welsh *f* (or *v*) being pronounced as an English *f* and written as *ff*.

Llandaf is the name of the cathedral church, 'the *llan* (church) on the river Taf'. Llandaf is an exceedingly old name. But *Caerdyf* must be older still. If it contains the form *Tyf*, it must go back to a very early period of the Welsh language – perhaps to the 6th century.[5]

cantref	district	*kann-trevv*

Cantref (central)

Welsh *cantref*, literally 'hundred townships', and roughly the same as an English administrative hundred. The parish Cantref derived its name from Cantref Mawr (Cantref Tewdos) in which it lay. The church was dedicated to St Cynidr, as at Llangynidr, which was replaced by Mary/Mair.[6]

Cantre'r Gwaelod

The legendary lands drowned under the rising western sea off the shore of Ceredigion. Lit. 'the bottom hundred townships'.

castell	castle	*kass-tell* (*ll* – see page 16)

Casnewydd (Newport)

The earliest form we have for the name of this town in Monmouthshire is *Novus Burgus* in a document of the year 1138. This is a Latin form, of course, comprising *novus*, 'new', and a Latinisation of the Old English word *burh* meaning 'town'.

Evidence of a submerged forest at Borth, near Aberystwyth – the memory of Cantre'r Gwaelod

Behind the *Novus Burgus* of the document was the English name *Newburh*, namely the 'new town' that was built by the Normans. The same elements *new* and *burh* gave Newbury in Berkshire its name; that was also a new town built in the time of the Normans.

In the case of the Monmouthshire town the second element *burh* was supplanted fairly early on by the word *port*, to give Newport. 'Town' or 'market town' was the meaning of *port* here, exactly as in the Newport on the Isle of Wight, and in the second part of Stockport.

The Welsh name was Castell Newydd ar Wysg ('new castle on the Usk'). That's how you find it spelt 600 years ago. In everyday speech *castell* at the beginning was abbreviated to *cas*. Castell Newydd became *Casnewydd*, just as Castell Gwent became *Cas-gwent*, Castell Llwchwr *Casllwchwr*, and the Pembrokeshire Castell Mael *Cas-mael*.

Newport is also the English name for the Pembrokeshire Trefdraeth. It's hard to be sure what *port* signifies in this name. It could mean 'town' or 'market town'. It could also have the sense 'harbour', as in Portsmouth. In the case of Newport in Monmouthshire there's scarcely any doubt. The old forms of the name show that *port* in the sense of 'town', 'market town' is what we have here.

cwrt	court	*kooert*
din	fort	*dinn*
dinas	fort, city	*dinnass*
ffordd	road	*forth*
heol	road	*hayoll*
llys	court	*thleess*

maer	stewart	*mire*

Maerdy (common throughout) Literally 'steward's house' with *maer* a chief officer or bailiff in a committee, later on manorial demesne, and *tŷ* which developed the sense 'dairy farm'.

neuadd	hall	*nayath*
pentref	village	*penn-trevv*
plas	mansion	*plahs* ('ah' as in 'ah!')
tai	houses	*tie*
tomen	mound	*tommenn*

Tredomen (central) 'Settlement by a mound', with *tref* as above and *tomen* (*tref* is feminine so *tomen* mutates to *domen*) 'mound', often 'castle mound'; there is a 'moat' at SN 119326.

tre	town	*tray*
tref	town	*trave*

Trecynon (south-eastern) '*tref* = originally 'house, dwelling-place, homestead', including the land held with the homestead; it developed the sense 'hamlet, village' probably at first to indicate 'the group of villein homesteads clustered together for the purpose of common cultivation of the surrounding land' and much later the modern sense 'town'. It also corresponds to English 'tun'.

Cynon – river name. The *tre* in *Trecynon* has the latest meaning of 'town'. *Trecynon* was submitted in an eisteddfod competition, in the 1850s, to devise an appropriate name for the mid 19th-century constructed 'suburb', and was later accepted as official appellation.[3]

Towns

Trefyclo (Knighton)

Trefyclo (Knighton) is a border town in Radnorshire. The name states that clearly enough: the old form was *Trefyclawdd* –i.e. the town that was on Offa's Dyke (*Clawdd*).

It seems that the name was originally *Tref-y-Clawdd*, in three parts, but in the course of time it came to be pronounced as a single word with the accent on the *y*, in accordance with the Welsh-language custom of accenting the penultimate syllable. The next natural step was the dropping of the final soft *dd* and the sounding of the *aw* as *o*. *Trefyclawdd* became *Trefýclo*, just as *Abermawdd* became *Amérmo* or *Bermo*.

Its English name *Knighton* is very old, going back a thousand years. It's a combination of two Old English words – *cniht*, meaning 'servant' or 'soldier', and *tun*, 'farm' etc., which gave *ton* at the end of so many English place names.

'Town of the soldiers' was the original meaning of Knighton. Incidentally, the same English word *cniht* – the old form of 'knight' – gave the Cnicht mountain in Meirionnydd its name: the shape of it resembles a knight's helmet.[5]

Laugharne (Welsh: Talacharn) (south-western) The medieval commote's name was transferred to the town at an early date. The element *tal* in the Welsh name means 'end/at the head of'. Suggestions

The old market hall at Llanidloes

regarding 'Lacharn' include *llachar* (light/gleaming) and *carn* (cairn). The original Welsh name was 'Normanized' with the loss of the unstressed 'Ta' (possibly through confusion with the French 'de').

It's a small town in Carmarthenshire, on a minor road on the Taf estuary, reached on the B4312 from Carmarthen.

In 1928, Dylan Thomas (1914–53) and his wife Caitlin came to live in a two-roomed cottage at 2 Gosport Street and then at Sea View, near the town hall and castle. They left in October of the same year but returned in 1949 to live at The Boathouse, a three-storey, whitewashed, slate-roofed cottage below the cliff, where the poet worked in a shed, formerly a garage, at the top of the garden. Both shed and house, which was opened as a museum in 1975, can be seen from the end of Cliff Road, renamed Dylan's Walk. Much of the writer's best work was done in Laugharne, including the greater part of his play for voices, *Under Milk Wood* (1954). The town of Llareggub (a name which requires to be read backwards) is usually said to be Laugharne, where the play has been performed regularly since 1958. Its opening words are: 'To begin at the beginning. It is spring, moonless night in the small town, starless and bible-black, the cobblestreets silent and the hunched, courters'-and-rabbits' wood limping invisible down to the sloeblack, slow, black, crowblack, fishingboat-bobbing sea.' It also includes the oft-quoted verse, spoken by the Reverend Eli Jenkins:

We are not wholly bad or good
Who live our lives under Milk Wood,

> And Thou, I know, wilt be the first
> To see our best side, not our worst.

After the writer's death on a reading tour of the USA on 9 November 1953, his body was brought home for burial in the annexe to the graveyard of St Martin's Church, where his grave is marked by a simple white wooden cross on which are painted his name and the date of his death. His parents were living at the time of his death at The Pelican, a house in King Street, and the poet's body rested there before his funeral. Among the other buildings associated with Dylan Thomas is Brown's, also in King Street, which was one of his favourite drinking places; the pub has a 'Dylan Thomas Corner'.

Sources

1. *Wales: a Celebration; an Anthology of Poetry and Prose*, ed. Dewi Roberts, Gwasg Carreg Gwalch, 2000.
2. *Pronouncing Welsh Place Names*, Tony Leaver, Gwasg Carreg Gwalch, 1998.
3. *Cynon Valley Place-names*, Deric John, Gwasg Carreg Gwalch, 1998.
4. *Place-names of Dee and Alun*, Hywel Wyn Owen, Gwasg Carreg Gwalch, 1996.
5. *Place-name Detective*, Bedwyr Lewis Jones (tr. Anthony Lias), Gwasg Carreg Gwalch, 2008.
6. *A Study of Breconshire Place-names*, Richard Morgan & R. F. Peter Powell, Gwasg Carreg Gwalch, 1999.
7. *A Guide to Welsh Place-names*, Anthony Lias, Gwasg Carreg Gwalch, 1994.
8. *Welsh Origins of Scottish Place-names*, William Oxenham, Gwasg Carreg Gwalch, 2005.
9. *Place-names in the 3000ft Mountains of Wales*, Terry Batt, Gwasg Carreg Gwalch, 1994.
10. *The Phenomenon of Welshness II*, Siôn Jobbins, Gwasg Carreg Gwalch, 2013.
11. *A Study of Montgomeryshire Place-names*, Richard Morgan, Gwasg Carreg Gwalch, 2001.
12. *A Study of Radnorshire Place-names*, Richard Morgan, Gwasg Carreg Gwalch, 1998.
13. *Place-names of Gwent*, Richard Morgan, Gwasg Carreg Gwalch, 2005.
14. *Herefordshire, the Welsh Connection*, Colin Lewis, Gwasg Carreg Gwalch, 2006.
15. *The Literary Pilgrim in Wales*, Meic Stephens, a guide to the places associated with writers in Wales, Gwasg Carreg Gwalch, 2000.
16. *Voyages of the Celtic Saints*, Graham Panes, Gwasg Carreg Gwalch, 2007.